"Success Habits: Achieving Your Goals through Daily Routines"

Introduction: In today's fast-paced world, achieving success often seems like a distant dream. However, success isn't just about luck or talent- it's about cultivating the right habits and consistently practicing them. This Book aims to guide you through practical daily habits that can significantly impact your journey towards success.

Content

- Understanding habits: How they form and influence our daily lives.
- The science behind habit formation and why it matters for success.
- Identifying your current habits and their impact on your goals.

Chapter 2: Setting Clear Goals
Pg No 8

- Defining success: What does it mean to you?
- The importance of setting SMART goals (Specific, Measurable, Achievable, Relevant, Time-bound).
- Creating a vision board or journal to visualize your goals daily.

Chapter 3: Morning Rituals for Success
Pg No 12

- The importance of a morning routine: Setting the tone for the day.
- Examples of effective morning habits: Meditation, exercise, gratitude practice.
- Tips for creating your personalized morning ritual that aligns with your goals.

Chapter 4: Productivity and Time Management
Pg No 18

- Strategies to optimize your daily schedule for maximum productivity.
- Prioritization techniques: Eisenhower Matrix, Pomodoro Technique, etc.
- The role of focus and concentration in achieving long-term goals.

Chapter 5: Healthy Mind, Healthy Body
Pg No 27

- The connection between physical health and mental clarity.
- Establishing habits for physical well-being: Exercise, nutrition, adequate sleep.
- Mindfulness and stress management techniques to enhance resilience.

Chapter 6: Continuous Learning and Growth

- The importance of lifelong learning in personal and professional development.
- Daily habits for learning: Reading, listening to podcasts, taking online courses.
- Cultivating a growth mindset: Embracing challenges and setbacks as opportunities for growth.

Chapter 7: Building Relationships and Networks

- The value of networking and fostering meaningful relationships.
- Daily habits for effective communication and relationship building.
- Strategies for expanding your professional network and leveraging it for success.

Chapter 8: Reflection and Adaptation

- The role of self-reflection in evaluating progress and adjusting course.
- Daily practices for self-assessment and course correction.
- Celebrating successes and learning from failures to fuel continuous improvement.

This Book provides a structured approach to achieving success through daily habits, offering practical advice and actionable steps that readers can implement immediately. By focusing on habits that foster productivity, well-being, and personal growth, readers can empower themselves to make positive changes and move closer to their goals each day.

Chapter 1: The Power of Habits

Understanding Habits: How They Form and Influence Our Daily Lives

Habits are integral to our daily lives, shaping our routines, decisions, and ultimately, our character. From the mundane rituals of brushing teeth in the morning to the complex behaviors of professional athletes, habits influence us profoundly. Understanding how habits form and their impact is crucial for personal development and achieving goals.

Formation of Habits:

Habits emerge through a neurological loop consisting of three stages: cue, routine, and reward, as described by Charles Duhigg in "The Power of Habit." The cue triggers a craving, which motivates the routine behavior, leading to the reward that satisfies the craving. This loop is reinforced through repetition, eventually becoming automatic. For instance, the sight of a toothbrush (cue) triggers the routine of brushing teeth, followed by the reward of clean teeth and fresh breath.

Moreover, habits are cemented through neuroplasticity, the brain's ability to reorganize itself based on experiences. Each repetition strengthens neural pathways associated with the habit, making it easier to perform over time. This explains why habits, whether positive or negative, become ingrained in our daily lives.

Influence on Daily Lives:

Habits permeate every aspect of our existence, influencing productivity, health, relationships, and overall well-being. Positive habits like regular exercise, healthy eating, and reading enhance physical and mental health, while negative habits such as procrastination or overindulgence in unhealthy substances can detract from our goals and happiness.

Furthermore, habits contribute to the formation of our identities and societal roles. A disciplined individual is often perceived as reliable, while someone with erratic habits may struggle to maintain relationships or professional success. Understanding and managing habits, therefore, is key to personal growth and social integration.

Changing Habits:

Although habits seem indomitable, they can be altered through conscious effort and understanding. The process involves identifying the cue-routine-reward cycle, replacing negative routines with positive alternatives, and reinforcing the desired behavior. For instance, replacing late-night snacking with herbal tea (alternative routine) can still provide comfort (reward) without the excess calories.

Additionally, leveraging social and environmental cues can facilitate habit change. Joining a gym or enlisting a workout buddy can encourage regular exercise by associating the cue of gym proximity with the routine of physical activity.

Conclusion:

In conclusion, habits are the building blocks of our daily lives, formed through repetitive behaviors and neurological processes. They influence our choices, behaviors, and ultimately shape our personal and professional outcomes. Understanding how habits form and affect us empowers individuals to cultivate positive behaviors and discard harmful ones, leading to a more fulfilling and productive life. By harnessing the power of habits, we can steer ourselves towards success, happiness, and a meaningful existence.

Thus, whether aiming to enhance health, achieve professional milestones, or strengthen relationships, the mastery of habits is fundamental to personal growth and lifelong fulfillment.

The Science Behind Habit Formation and Why It Matters for Success

Habits are the invisible architects of our lives, influencing our daily routines, decisions, and ultimately, our success. Understanding the science behind habit formation offers profound insights into how we can shape our behaviors and achieve our goals effectively.

Neurological Basis of Habit Formation:

At the core of habit formation lies the brain's ability to create neural pathways that reinforce behaviors through repetition. The process involves a loop of cue, routine, and reward. When we encounter a cue (such as feeling stressed), our brain initiates a routine (like eating comfort food), which results in a reward (temporary relief). Each repetition strengthens this loop, making the behavior more automatic and less reliant on conscious decision-making.

Neuroscientists have identified the basal ganglia as a key player in habit formation. This brain region coordinates routines and automates behaviors to conserve cognitive resources. By understanding this process, individuals can strategically form new habits that align with their goals, whether in personal development, professional achievement, or health improvement.

Importance of Habit Formation for Success:

Successful individuals often attribute their achievements to disciplined habits. Whether in business, athletics, or academics, habits streamline actions, foster consistency, and mitigate decision fatigue. For instance, a successful entrepreneur may credit their habit of daily planning and prioritization for their ability to navigate challenges effectively and stay focused on long-term goals.

Moreover, habits cultivate a growth mindset by reinforcing positive behaviors and fostering resilience. Consistently practicing skills or routines builds competence and confidence over time, crucial for mastering complex tasks or overcoming setbacks. Athletes, for example, rely on training habits to optimize performance under pressure, demonstrating the transformative power of habitual excellence.

Strategies for Cultivating Successful Habits:

Changing habits requires understanding the cues triggering undesired behaviors and strategically replacing them with constructive routines. This process involves:

1. **Identifying Triggers:** Recognizing cues (time of day, emotional states, environment) that prompt habitual behaviors.
2. **Introducing New Routines:** Substituting old routines with positive alternatives that align with goals. For instance, replacing procrastination with structured time management techniques.
3. **Reinforcing Rewards:** Ensuring new behaviors yield satisfying rewards, reinforcing the habit loop. This could involve celebrating small wins or acknowledging progress towards larger objectives.
4. **Building Consistency:** Practicing new habits consistently to solidify neural pathways and make desired behaviors automatic.

Application Across Domains:

The impact of habit formation extends across various domains of life. In education, students benefit from study habits that promote effective learning and academic success. In health and fitness, adopting routines like regular exercise or nutritious eating supports physical well-being. Professionally, habits such as networking, continuous learning, and prioritization contribute to career advancement and leadership development.

Conclusion:

In conclusion, the science behind habit formation underscores its critical role in achieving success. By harnessing neuroplasticity and understanding the habit loop, individuals can cultivate behaviors that drive progress and personal fulfillment. Successful habit formation involves deliberate practice, resilience in the face of setbacks, and a commitment to continuous improvement.

Ultimately, habits shape our identities and determine our trajectories. Whether aiming for professional excellence, personal growth, or a balanced lifestyle, mastering the science of habit formation empowers individuals to navigate challenges effectively and maximize their potential. As we continue to unravel the complexities of human behavior, harnessing the power of habits remains a cornerstone of success in all its forms.

Identifying Your Current Habits and Their Impact on Your Goals

Habits are the silent architects of our lives, shaping our routines, decisions, and ultimately, our achievements. Identifying and understanding our current habits is crucial for aligning our behaviors with our goals, whether personal, professional, or academic. By examining how our habits influence our daily lives, we can effectively chart a path towards success and fulfillment.

Understanding Current Habits:

Our habits encompass a wide range of behaviors, from simple routines like waking up at a certain time to complex patterns such as how we manage stress or approach tasks. These habits are often ingrained through repetition and serve as automatic responses to cues in our environment or emotions.

To identify our current habits, it's essential to observe our daily routines objectively. This involves:

1. **Self-awareness:** Paying attention to our actions and reactions throughout the day. Are there patterns that recur consistently?
2. **Tracking behaviors:** Keeping a journal or using habit-tracking apps to record activities and their triggers. This helps in pinpointing specific habits and understanding what prompts them.
3. **Reflecting on outcomes:** Assessing the consequences of our habits. Do they contribute positively or hinder progress towards our goals? For instance, procrastination might delay deadlines and affect productivity.

Impact of Habits on Goals:

Our habits exert a profound influence on the outcomes we achieve in various areas of life. Positive habits, such as regular exercise or maintaining a healthy diet, contribute to physical well-being and long-term health goals. Similarly, habits like effective time management or continuous learning bolster professional growth and career advancement.

Conversely, negative habits can act as barriers to success. These might include habits of self-doubt, avoidance of challenges, or unhealthy coping mechanisms. Identifying these habits allows us to address their impact on our goals and take proactive steps towards change.

Aligning Habits with Goals:

Once identified, aligning our habits with our goals involves intentional and strategic adjustments:

1. **Goal clarification:** Clearly defining short-term and long-term goals in different areas of life (career, health, relationships).
2. **Mapping habits to goals:** Assessing whether current habits support or hinder these goals. If a goal is to improve productivity, habits like minimizing distractions and setting daily priorities would be beneficial.
3. **Implementing change:** Introducing new habits that reinforce desired outcomes. This might involve setting specific routines, seeking accountability, or creating supportive environments conducive to change.
4. **Monitoring progress:** Regularly reviewing habits and their impact on goal achievement. Adjusting strategies as needed to maintain momentum and overcome obstacles.

Case Studies and Examples:

Consider successful individuals across various fields. Entrepreneurs often credit habits like strategic planning, networking, and resilience in adversity for their achievements. Athletes rely on disciplined training routines and mental preparation to excel in competitions. Academics cultivate habits of continuous learning and effective study techniques to excel in their disciplines.

Conclusion:

In conclusion, identifying our current habits and their impact on our goals is a foundational step towards personal growth and success. By gaining awareness of our behaviors, we empower ourselves to make informed decisions and cultivate habits that align with our aspirations. Whether aiming for career advancement, health improvement, or personal development, understanding the role of habits equips us to navigate challenges effectively and maximize our potential.

Ultimately, habits are not just routines; they are powerful tools that shape our destinies. Through introspection, deliberate action, and persistence, we can harness the transformative power of habits to create a life filled with purpose, achievement, and fulfillment.

Chapter 2: Setting Clear Goals

- Defining success: What does it mean to you?
- The importance of setting SMART goals (Specific, Measurable, Achievable, Relevant, Time-bound).
- Creating a vision board or journal to visualize your goals daily.

Defining success: What does it mean to you?

Defining success is a deeply personal endeavor, shaped by individual values, aspirations, and life experiences. For me, success transcends mere achievement or material wealth; it encompasses a holistic sense of fulfillment and purpose in various aspects of life.

1. **Personal Fulfillment:** Success, to me, means finding joy and satisfaction in what I do—whether it's pursuing a career that aligns with my passions, cultivating meaningful relationships, or engaging in activities that nourish my soul. It involves striving towards personal growth and self-acceptance, continuously evolving into the best version of myself.

2. **Impact and Contribution:** Success also involves making a positive impact on others and the world around me. It means contributing to the well-being of society, whether through acts of kindness, sharing knowledge, or actively participating in initiatives that promote social justice and equality.

3. **Professional Achievement:** While career success is important, it goes beyond financial rewards or status. It includes achieving professional goals that are meaningful to me, such as making a difference in my field, leading by example, and inspiring others through my work.

4. **Balance and Well-being:** True success, in my view, encompasses a balanced life where I prioritize my physical, mental, and emotional well-being. It involves nurturing relationships with loved ones, maintaining a healthy lifestyle, and finding harmony between work and leisure.

5. **Continuous Learning and Growth:** Success is a journey rather than a destination. It involves embracing challenges, learning from failures, and constantly expanding my knowledge and skills. It means being open to new experiences and seizing opportunities for personal and professional development.

6. **Authenticity and Integrity:** Ultimately, success is about living authentically and in alignment with my values. It means staying true to myself, acting with integrity, and having the courage to follow my dreams even in the face of adversity.

In essence, defining success for me is about leading a purposeful life, making a positive impact, and finding fulfillment in both my personal journey and contributions to the world. It's about striving for excellence while maintaining a sense of gratitude and humility along the way. Success, therefore, is not static but dynamic—a continuous pursuit of growth, happiness, and making a meaningful difference in the lives of others.

The importance of setting SMART goals (Specific, Measurable, Achievable, Relevant, Time-bound).

Setting SMART goals is crucial for both personal and professional development because it ensures that objectives are clear, trackable, realistic, aligned with broader aims, and time-sensitive. Here's a breakdown of the importance of each element of SMART goals:

Specific

- **Clarity**: A specific goal is clear and unambiguous, which reduces confusion and provides a clear direction.
- **Focus**: It narrows down what needs to be achieved, making it easier to focus efforts and resources effectively.

Measurable

- **Tracking Progress**: A measurable goal allows you to track progress and measure outcomes, providing tangible evidence of success or identifying areas needing improvement.
- **Motivation**: Seeing measurable progress can boost motivation and encourage continued effort toward the goal.

Achievable

- **Realism**: An achievable goal is realistic and attainable, considering current resources and constraints, which prevents setting goals that are too lofty and potentially discouraging.

- **Challenge**: It should still be challenging enough to push you out of your comfort zone and promote growth and development.

Relevant

- **Alignment**: A relevant goal aligns with broader objectives, whether personal or organizational, ensuring that the efforts contribute to overall aims.
- **Significance**: It emphasizes the importance of the goal, ensuring that it matters to the individual or organization, which can increase commitment and effort.

Time-bound

- **Deadline**: A time-bound goal has a clear deadline, which creates a sense of urgency and helps prioritize tasks.
- **Time Management**: It encourages efficient use of time and resources, preventing procrastination and ensuring steady progress.

Overall Benefits

- **Enhanced Productivity**: SMART goals provide a clear roadmap, helping to enhance productivity by ensuring focused and efficient efforts.
- **Improved Performance**: Regular tracking and reassessment of goals can lead to improved performance and higher chances of success.
- **Motivation and Engagement**: Clear, attainable goals can boost motivation and engagement, as individuals see the impact of their efforts and feel a sense of accomplishment.

By incorporating these elements, SMART goals provide a structured and clear approach to goal-setting that can significantly improve the chances of achieving desired outcomes.

Creating a vision board or journal to visualize your goals daily.

Creating a vision board or journal to visualize your goals daily is a powerful tool for maintaining focus, motivation, and clarity. Here's how each method can help you achieve your goals:

Vision Board

Benefits:

- **Visualization**: Seeing your goals represented visually every day can reinforce your commitment and keep your objectives top of mind.
- **Inspiration**: A vision board filled with images, quotes, and affirmations that resonate with your goals can inspire and uplift you, especially during challenging times.
- **Clarity**: It helps clarify your vision by requiring you to define what you truly want, making your goals more tangible and concrete.
- **Focus**: It serves as a constant reminder of what you are working towards, helping to maintain focus and avoid distractions.

How to Create a Vision Board:

1. **Gather Materials**: Collect magazines, photos, quotes, and other visual elements that represent your goals.
2. **Define Your Goals**: Be clear about what you want to achieve in various areas of your life, such as career, health, relationships, and personal growth.
3. **Arrange the Images**: Place the images and quotes on a board in a way that is visually appealing and meaningful to you.
4. **Display**: Put the vision board in a place where you will see it daily, such as your bedroom, office, or a frequently used space.

Journal

- **Reflection**: Journaling allows for regular reflection on your progress, challenges, and achievements, helping you stay aligned with your goals.
- **Detailing Plans**: You can outline detailed action plans, break down goals into manageable steps, and track your daily or weekly progress.
- **Flexibility**: A journal provides flexibility to adapt and modify your goals as circumstances change or as you grow and learn.
- **Emotional Outlet**: Writing can serve as an emotional outlet, helping you process thoughts and feelings related to your goals and journey.

How to Maintain a Goal Journal:

1. **Set Up**: Choose a journal that you enjoy using, whether it's a physical notebook or a digital app.
2. **Define Your Goals**: Clearly outline your SMART goals in the journal.
3. **Daily Entries**: Write daily or regular entries reflecting on your progress, challenges, and next steps.
4. **Review and Adjust**: Periodically review your goals and progress, making adjustments as necessary to stay on track.

Combined Approach

- **Synergy**: Combining both a vision board and a journal can create a powerful synergy. The vision board keeps your goals visually present, while the journal allows for detailed planning and reflection.
- **Complementary Tools**: Use the vision board for inspiration and big-picture visualization, and the journal for actionable steps, detailed tracking, and deeper introspection.

Tips for Success

- **Consistency**: Make it a habit to engage with your vision board and journal daily. Consistency is key to staying connected with your goals.
- **Positivity**: Keep the tone positive and focused on what you want to achieve, rather than on what you want to avoid.
- **Celebrate**: Celebrate small victories along the way to stay motivated and acknowledge your progress.

By incorporating these tools into your daily routine, you can maintain a clear focus on your goals, stay motivated, and effectively track your journey toward achieving them.

Chapter 3: Morning Rituals for Success

- The importance of a morning routine: Setting the tone for the day.
- Examples of effective morning habits: Meditation, exercise, gratitude practice.
- Tips for creating your personalized morning ritual that aligns with your goals.

The importance of a morning routine: Setting the tone for the day.

A well-crafted morning routine is crucial for setting the tone for the day, influencing your mood, productivity, and overall well-being. Here are several key reasons why a morning routine is important:

1. Increases Productivity

- **Preparation**: Starting the day with a structured routine helps you prepare mentally and physically for the tasks ahead.

- **Focus**: Establishing clear priorities in the morning can lead to greater focus and efficiency throughout the day.

2. Enhances Mental Clarity

- **Mindfulness**: Incorporating mindfulness practices such as meditation or journaling can clear your mind and reduce stress.
- **Planning**: Taking time to plan your day can provide a clear roadmap, reducing decision fatigue and increasing clarity.

3. Boosts Physical Health

- **Exercise**: Morning exercise can boost your energy levels, improve mood, and enhance overall physical health.
- **Nutrition**: A healthy breakfast can fuel your body and brain, setting a positive tone for the day.

4. Improves Emotional Well-being

- **Positive Start**: Engaging in activities that you enjoy or find fulfilling can improve your mood and set a positive emotional tone.
- **Gratitude**: Practicing gratitude in the morning can foster a positive outlook and improve emotional resilience.

5. Builds Consistency and Discipline

- **Routine**: Establishing a consistent morning routine can create a sense of stability and discipline, which can positively impact other areas of your life.
- **Habits**: Regularly performing positive habits in the morning can make them more likely to stick, leading to long-term benefits.

6. Reduces Stress

- **Control**: Starting the day with a routine gives you a sense of control, reducing anxiety and stress.
- **Calm**: A calm, unhurried start can set a peaceful tone for the rest of the day.

Key Components of an Effective Morning Routine

1. **Wake Up Early**: Allow yourself ample time to engage in your routine without feeling rushed.
2. **Hydrate**: Drink a glass of water to kickstart your metabolism and hydrate your body.
3. **Exercise**: Engage in physical activity to boost energy and improve mood.
4. **Mindfulness or Meditation**: Practice mindfulness, meditation, or deep breathing to enhance mental clarity and reduce stress.
5. **Healthy Breakfast**: Eat a nutritious breakfast to fuel your body and brain.
6. **Personal Development**: Spend time reading, journaling, or learning something new to foster personal growth.
7. **Plan Your Day**: Outline your key tasks and priorities to create a clear roadmap for the day.

Tips for Success

- **Start Small**: Begin with a few key activities and gradually build your routine.
- **Be Consistent**: Try to maintain your routine even on weekends to build a consistent habit.
- **Adjust as Needed**: Tailor your routine to fit your lifestyle and preferences, making adjustments as necessary.

Example Morning Routine

1. **Wake Up at 6:00 AM**
2. **Hydrate with a Glass of Water**
3. **20-Minute Exercise (e.g., Yoga, Jogging)**
4. **10-Minute Meditation**

5. **Healthy Breakfast (e.g., Smoothie, Oatmeal)**
6. **Read for 15 Minutes**
7. **Journal for 10 Minutes**
8. **Plan the Day (Review To-Do List and Priorities)**

By establishing a consistent and positive morning routine, you can set the tone for a productive, focused, and fulfilling day, ultimately contributing to your overall well-being and success.

Examples of effective morning habits: Meditation, exercise, gratitude practice.

Implementing effective morning habits can significantly enhance your productivity, mood, and overall well-being. Here are examples of three powerful morning habits—meditation, exercise, and gratitude practice—along with tips on how to incorporate them into your daily routine:

1. Meditation

Benefits:

- **Reduces Stress**: Helps lower stress levels and promotes a sense of calm and relaxation.
- **Enhances Focus**: Improves concentration and mental clarity.
- **Boosts Emotional Health**: Increases self-awareness and emotional well-being.

How to Incorporate Meditation:

1. **Choose a Quiet Space**: Find a quiet, comfortable place where you won't be disturbed.
2. **Set a Time Limit**: Start with 5-10 minutes and gradually increase as you become more comfortable.
3. **Focus on Your Breath**: Close your eyes and focus on your breathing. Inhale deeply and exhale slowly.

4. **Use Guided Meditations**: Consider using apps like Headspace, Calm, or Insight Timer for guided sessions.
5. **Be Consistent**: Try to meditate at the same time each morning to build a habit.

Example:

- **5-Minute Meditation**: Sit comfortably, close your eyes, and focus on your breath for five minutes. If your mind wanders, gently bring your focus back to your breathing.

2. Exercise

Benefits:

- **Boosts Energy**: Increases energy levels and improves overall physical health.
- **Enhances Mood**: Releases endorphins that improve mood and reduce feelings of anxiety and depression.
- **Improves Focus**: Enhances cognitive function and focus for the day ahead.

How to Incorporate Exercise:

1. **Choose an Activity You Enjoy**: Whether it's jogging, yoga, cycling, or a home workout, pick something you like.
2. **Set a Time**: Dedicate a specific time each morning for exercise, even if it's just 15-30 minutes.
3. **Prepare in Advance**: Lay out your workout clothes and equipment the night before.
4. **Mix It Up**: Vary your routine to keep it interesting and work different muscle groups.

Example:

- **20-Minute Morning Workout**:
  - 5 minutes of warm-up (stretching or light jogging)
  - 10 minutes of moderate exercise (e.g., jumping jacks, push-ups, squats)

- o 5 minutes of cool-down (stretching or yoga poses)

3. Gratitude Practice

Benefits:

- **Increases Positivity**: Focusing on what you're grateful for can boost happiness and positivity.
- **Reduces Stress**: Shifts your focus from negative to positive aspects of your life.
- **Enhances Well-being**: Promotes overall emotional well-being and resilience.

How to Incorporate Gratitude Practice:

1. **Keep a Gratitude Journal**: Write down 3-5 things you are grateful for each morning.
2. **Be Specific**: Specify why you are grateful for each item to deepen the practice.
3. **Consistency**: Make it a daily habit, preferably at the same time each morning.
4. **Reflect on Your Entries**: Occasionally review your past entries to remind yourself of positive experiences and accomplishments.

Example:

- **Morning Gratitude Journal**: Spend 5 minutes each morning writing down three things you are grateful for and why. For example, "I am grateful for my supportive partner because they always encourage me to pursue my goals."

Integrating These Habits into a Morning Routine

Sample Morning Routine:

1. **6:00 AM**: Wake up and drink a glass of water.
2. **6:10 AM**: 5-minute meditation session.
3. **6:20 AM**: 20-minute exercise (e.g., yoga, jogging, or a home workout).

4. **6:45 AM**: Shower and get dressed.
5. **7:00 AM**: Healthy breakfast.
6. **7:15 AM**: Spend 5 minutes writing in your gratitude journal.
7. **7:30 AM**: Review your plans and priorities for the day.

By consistently incorporating these habits into your morning routine, you can set a positive and productive tone for the rest of the day, enhancing your overall well-being and helping you achieve your goals.

Tips for creating your personalized morning ritual that aligns with your goals

Creating a personalized morning ritual that aligns with your goals involves understanding your priorities, preferences, and the actions that best support your aspirations. Here are some tips to help you design a morning ritual that suits your needs and enhances your daily life:

1. Identify Your Goals

- **Clarify Objectives**: Determine what you want to achieve in the short term and long term. This could be related to health, career, personal growth, relationships, or any other area of life.
- **Align Activities**: Choose morning activities that directly support these goals. For example, if improving fitness is a goal, include exercise in your morning routine.

2. Prioritize Key Activities

- **Essential Tasks**: Focus on the most impactful activities that set a positive tone for the day. This could be meditation, exercise, reading, or planning your day.
- **Avoid Overloading**: Don't try to do too much. Select a few key activities that you can consistently maintain.

3. Consider Your Preferences and Lifestyle

- **Personal Enjoyment**: Choose activities you enjoy and look forward to. This increases the likelihood of sticking to your routine.
- **Feasibility**: Ensure your morning ritual fits within the time you have available. Adjust wake-up times if necessary to accommodate your chosen activities.

4. Create a Structured Plan

- **Set a Schedule**: Allocate specific times for each activity. A structured plan helps you stay on track and ensures you cover all essential tasks.
- **Be Flexible**: Allow for some flexibility to adapt to changes in your schedule or unexpected events.

5. Start Small and Build Gradually

- **Begin with Essentials**: Start with a few core activities and gradually add more as you become comfortable with your routine.
- **Incremental Changes**: Slowly increase the duration or intensity of activities, such as extending meditation time or increasing workout intensity.

6. Prepare the Night Before

- **Lay Out Clothes and Equipment**: Prepare workout clothes, meditation cushions, or any tools you'll need in the morning.
- **Plan Your Day**: Spend a few minutes the night before organizing your tasks and priorities for the next day.

7. Incorporate Reflection and Adjustment

- **Review Your Routine**: Regularly assess how well your morning ritual is working. Reflect on what's effective and what needs adjustment.
- **Be Adaptable**: Don't be afraid to tweak your routine based on what you learn about your preferences and what helps you achieve your goals.

8. Stay Consistent

- **Build Habits**: Consistency is key to forming lasting habits. Try to perform your morning ritual at the same time every day.
- **Patience and Persistence**: Building a new routine takes time. Be patient and persistent, even if you miss a day or two.

Example Personalized Morning Ritual

1. **6:00 AM**: Wake up and drink a glass of water.
2. **6:05 AM**: 5 minutes of stretching or light yoga to wake up the body.
3. **6:10 AM**: 10 minutes of meditation or deep breathing exercises.
4. **6:20 AM**: 20-minute workout (e.g., jogging, home workout, or gym session).
5. **6:40 AM**: Shower and get dressed.
6. **7:00 AM**: Healthy breakfast.
7. **7:15 AM**: Spend 10 minutes journaling or writing down three things you're grateful for.
8. **7:25 AM**: Review your goals and to-do list for the day.

By creating a morning ritual that aligns with your goals, you can start each day with intention, clarity, and motivation, ultimately leading to a more productive and fulfilling life.

Chapter 4: Productivity and Time Management

- Strategies to optimize your daily schedule for maximum productivity.
- Prioritization techniques: Eisenhower Matrix, Pomodoro Technique, etc.
- The role of focus and concentration in achieving long-term goals.

Strategies to optimize your daily schedule for maximum productivity.

Optimizing your daily schedule for maximum productivity involves strategic planning, effective time management, and prioritization of tasks. Here are several strategies to help you achieve this:

1. Prioritize Tasks Using the Eisenhower Matrix

- **Urgent and Important**: Do these tasks first.
- **Important but Not Urgent**: Schedule these tasks.
- **Urgent but Not Important**: Delegate these tasks.
- **Not Urgent and Not Important**: Eliminate or minimize these tasks.

2. Time Blocking

- **Set Specific Time Blocks**: Allocate dedicated time blocks for specific tasks or groups of tasks.
- **Include Breaks**: Schedule regular breaks to prevent burnout and maintain focus.
- **Batch Similar Tasks**: Group similar tasks together to minimize context switching and increase efficiency.

3. Utilize the Pomodoro Technique

- **Work in Intervals**: Work for 25 minutes (a "Pomodoro") and then take a 5-minute break.
- **Longer Breaks**: After completing four Pomodoros, take a longer break (15-30 minutes).
- **Stay Focused**: During each Pomodoro, focus solely on the task at hand.

4. Set Clear Goals and Objectives

- **Daily Goals**: Define specific, achievable goals for each day.
- **Weekly Planning**: Review and adjust your weekly goals to ensure alignment with long-term objectives.
- **SMART Goals**: Ensure your goals are Specific, Measurable, Achievable, Relevant, and Time-bound.

5. Prioritize High-Energy Tasks

- **Peak Productivity Times**: Identify when you are most productive during the day and schedule high-priority tasks during these times.
- **Low-Energy Periods**: Use less productive times for routine or less demanding tasks.

6. Minimize Distractions

- **Environment**: Create a workspace free from distractions.

- **Digital Distractions**: Use apps or browser extensions to block distracting websites and notifications during work periods.
- **Set Boundaries**: Let others know your work schedule to minimize interruptions.

7. Implement the Two-Minute Rule

- **Quick Tasks**: If a task can be completed in two minutes or less, do it immediately.
- **Prevent Procrastination**: This helps prevent small tasks from piling up and becoming overwhelming.

8. Review and Reflect Daily

- **End-of-Day Review**: Spend a few minutes at the end of each day reviewing what you've accomplished.
- **Adjust Tomorrow's Plan**: Adjust your schedule and tasks for the next day based on what you completed and any new priorities.

9. Use Productivity Tools and Apps

- **Task Management**: Use apps like Todoist, Trello, or Asana to manage and track tasks.
- **Time Management**: Use time-tracking tools like Toggl or RescueTime to monitor how you spend your time.
- **Digital Calendars**: Use digital calendars to schedule tasks and set reminders.

10. Delegate and Outsource

- **Identify Tasks to Delegate**: Determine which tasks can be delegated to others.
- **Leverage Outsourcing**: Outsource tasks that others can do more efficiently or that do not require your specific expertise.

11. Maintain Work-Life Balance

- **Set Boundaries**: Clearly define your working hours and stick to them.
- **Personal Time**: Schedule time for relaxation, hobbies, and spending time with loved ones.
- **Self-Care**: Ensure you get enough sleep, eat healthily, and exercise regularly to maintain energy levels.

12. Continuous Improvement

- **Regular Reviews**: Regularly review and adjust your productivity strategies to see what works best for you.
- **Learn and Adapt**: Stay open to new techniques and tools that could enhance your productivity.

Example of an Optimized Daily Schedule

1. **6:00 AM**: Wake up, hydrate, and do a 10-minute stretch.
2. **6:10 AM**: 20-minute exercise routine.
3. **6:30 AM**: Shower and get dressed.
4. **7:00 AM**: Healthy breakfast.
5. **7:30 AM**: Review and finalize daily goals.
6. **8:00 AM**: Start work with high-priority tasks (time block until 10:00 AM).
7. **10:00 AM**: Take a 10-minute break.
8. **10:10 AM**: Continue work on secondary tasks (time block until 12:00 PM).
9. **12:00 PM**: Lunch break and short walk.
10. **1:00 PM**: Resume work with remaining tasks (time block until 3:00 PM).
11. **3:00 PM**: Take a 10-minute break.
12. **3:10 PM**: Respond to emails and administrative tasks.
13. **4:00 PM**: Wrap up the day with final review and plan for tomorrow.
14. **5:00 PM**: End workday and transition to personal time.

By following these strategies, you can optimize your daily schedule to maximize productivity, reduce stress, and achieve a better work-life balance.

Prioritization techniques: Eisenhower Matrix, Pomodoro Technique, etc.

Effective prioritization techniques are crucial for managing tasks efficiently and maximizing productivity. Here are detailed explanations and examples of several prioritization techniques, including the Eisenhower Matrix and the Pomodoro Technique:

1. Eisenhower Matrix (Urgent-Important Matrix)

The Eisenhower Matrix helps prioritize tasks based on their urgency and importance.

Quadrants:

1. **Urgent and Important**: Tasks that need immediate attention and have significant consequences if not completed.
2. **Important but Not Urgent**: Tasks that are important for long-term goals but do not require immediate action.
3. **Urgent but Not Important**: Tasks that need immediate attention but do not contribute significantly to long-term goals.
4. **Not Urgent and Not Important**: Tasks that have little impact and can often be eliminated or minimized.

How to Use:

- **List Tasks**: Write down all tasks.
- **Categorize**: Place each task in the appropriate quadrant.
- **Act Accordingly**:
    - **Quadrant 1**: Do these tasks first.
    - **Quadrant 2**: Schedule these tasks.
    - **Quadrant 3**: Delegate these tasks if possible.
    - **Quadrant 4**: Eliminate or minimize these tasks.

- **Urgent and Important**: Complete project due today.
- **Important but Not Urgent**: Plan next week's presentation.
- **Urgent but Not Important**: Reply to non-critical emails.
- **Not Urgent and Not Important**: Browse social media.

2. Pomodoro Technique

The Pomodoro Technique helps manage time and maintain focus by breaking work into intervals.

Steps:

1. **Choose a Task**: Select a task to work on.
2. **Set a Timer**: Set a timer for 25 minutes (one Pomodoro).
3. **Work on the Task**: Focus solely on the task until the timer goes off.
4. **Short Break**: Take a 5-minute break.
5. **Repeat**: Repeat the process four times, then take a longer break (15-30 minutes).

Benefits:

- **Improved Focus**: Short, timed work periods help maintain concentration.
- **Regular Breaks**: Frequent breaks prevent burnout and keep the mind fresh.

Example:

- **8:00 AM**: Start first Pomodoro on writing a report.
- **8:25 AM**: Take a 5-minute break.
- **8:30 AM**: Start second Pomodoro on the same task.
- **8:55 AM**: Take a 5-minute break.
- **9:00 AM**: Start third Pomodoro on another part of the report.
- **9:25 AM**: Take a 5-minute break.
- **9:30 AM**: Start fourth Pomodoro on reviewing the report.
- **9:55 AM**: Take a 15-30 minute break.

3. ABCDE Method

The ABCDE Method categorizes tasks based on their level of priority.

Steps:

1. **List Tasks**: Write down all tasks.
2. **Assign Letters**: Assign each task a letter from A to E:

- **A**: Very important, must be done.
- **B**: Important, should be done.
- **C**: Nice to do, but not necessary.
- **D**: Delegate to someone else.
- **E**: Eliminate if possible.

3. **Work in Order**: Start with A tasks before moving to B, and so on.

Example:

- **A**: Prepare for an important client meeting.
- **B**: Follow up on pending project approvals.
- **C**: Organize office files.
- **D**: Delegate routine data entry to an assistant.
- **E**: Eliminate unnecessary meetings.

4. Eat That Frog

The "Eat That Frog" technique emphasizes tackling the most challenging task first.

Steps:

1. **Identify the Frog**: Determine your most difficult or important task.
2. **Do It First**: Start your day by completing this task before anything else.

- **Reduces Procrastination**: Addresses the tendency to delay difficult tasks.
- **Boosts Productivity**: Completing the hardest task first can increase motivation for the rest of the day.

Example:

- **8:00 AM**: Work on the most challenging project of the day.
- **10:00 AM**: Move on to other tasks after completing the major one.

5. 1-3-5 Rule

The 1-3-5 Rule simplifies task prioritization by limiting the number of tasks.

Steps:

1. **Daily Plan**: Plan to accomplish one big task, three medium tasks, and five small tasks each day.
2. **List Tasks**: Write down your tasks according to these categories.

Example:

- **1 Big Task**: Finish the quarterly financial report.
- **3 Medium Tasks**: Prepare for a team meeting, review a project proposal, complete a client follow-up.
- **5 Small Tasks**: Respond to emails, update calendar, schedule appointments, read industry news, organize desk.

6. MoSCoW Method

The MoSCoW Method prioritizes tasks based on necessity.

Categories:

- **Must Have**: Essential tasks that are critical to complete.
- **Should Have**: Important tasks that are not critical but add significant value.
- **Could Have**: Nice-to-have tasks that are not essential.
- **Won't Have**: Tasks that are not a priority and can be deferred or eliminated.

Example:

- **Must Have**: Submit the project proposal by the deadline.
- **Should Have**: Update the project timeline.
- **Could Have**: Redesign the project template.
- **Won't Have**: Attend a non-essential meeting.

By applying these prioritization techniques, you can manage your tasks more effectively, reduce stress, and increase your overall productivity. Select the methods that resonate most with your work style and goals, and adapt them to suit your needs.

The role of focus and concentration in achieving long-term goals.

Focus and concentration are pivotal in achieving long-term goals. They enable sustained effort, efficient use of time, and resilience against distractions and setbacks. Here's an in-depth look at their role:

1. Sustained Effort and Consistency

Maintaining Progress

- **Regular Work**: Long-term goals require continuous effort over extended periods. Focus and concentration help maintain this steady progress.

- **Habit Formation**: Consistent focus on daily tasks leads to the formation of productive habits that support goal achievement.

Example

- **Learning a New Skill**: To master a musical instrument, daily practice sessions require intense concentration to improve over time.

2. Efficient Use of Time

Maximizing Productivity

- **Deep Work**: Engaging in deep, focused work sessions allows for higher productivity and the completion of complex tasks.
- **Avoiding Multitasking**: Concentration helps avoid multitasking, which can reduce efficiency and the quality of work.

Example

- **Writing a Book**: An author needs focused, uninterrupted writing sessions to produce high-quality content efficiently.

3. Overcoming Challenges and Setbacks

Resilience

- **Problem-Solving**: Concentration aids in tackling difficult problems and finding solutions.
- **Persistence**: Staying focused on long-term goals helps overcome obstacles and maintain motivation during tough times.

Example

- **Starting a Business**: Entrepreneurs face numerous challenges; maintaining focus on their vision helps navigate setbacks and stay committed.

4. Improved Quality of Work

Attention to Detail

- **Accuracy**: Concentration ensures that tasks are completed with attention to detail, reducing errors and enhancing the quality of outcomes.
- **Creativity and Innovation**: Deep focus can foster creativity and innovative thinking, which are crucial for achieving significant long-term goals.

Example

- **Scientific Research**: Researchers need to meticulously design experiments and analyze data, requiring sustained focus to produce reliable results.

5. Setting and Achieving Milestones

Strategic Planning

- **Breaking Down Goals**: Concentration helps in breaking down long-term goals into manageable milestones and setting realistic timelines.
- **Tracking Progress**: Regular focus sessions allow for the consistent tracking and reassessment of progress toward these milestones.

Example

- **Fitness Goals**: Achieving a long-term fitness goal, like running a marathon, requires setting and meeting incremental milestones in training.

6. Mindfulness and Mental Clarity

- **Mindfulness Practices**: Techniques like meditation enhance concentration and reduce stress, supporting long-term goal pursuit.
- **Mental Clarity**: A focused mind can make better decisions, prioritize effectively, and stay aligned with long-term objectives.

Example

- **Career Advancement**: Clarity in career goals and focused efforts on professional development can lead to significant career growth over time.

Strategies to Enhance Focus and Concentration

1. **Set Clear Goals**: Clearly define long-term goals and break them into smaller, manageable tasks.
2. **Create a Routine**: Establish a daily routine that includes dedicated time blocks for focused work.
3. **Eliminate Distractions**: Minimize external and internal distractions by creating a conducive work environment.
4. **Practice Mindfulness**: Engage in mindfulness practices such as meditation to improve concentration.
5. **Take Regular Breaks**: Use techniques like the Pomodoro Technique to balance focused work with short breaks.
6. **Stay Organized**: Keep a structured plan or to-do list to track progress and stay on course.
7. **Maintain Health**: Ensure adequate sleep, nutrition, and exercise to support cognitive function and concentration.

By maintaining focus and concentration, you can effectively manage the demands of long-term goals, stay motivated, and achieve success in your endeavors.

Chapter 5: Healthy Mind, Healthy Body

- The connection between physical health and mental clarity.
- Establishing habits for physical well-being: Exercise, nutrition, adequate sleep.

- Mindfulness and stress management techniques to enhance resilience.

The connection between physical health and mental clarity

Physical health and mental clarity are deeply interconnected. Maintaining good physical health can significantly enhance mental clarity, cognitive function, and overall psychological well-being. Here's a detailed exploration of this connection:

1. Exercise and Cognitive Function

Improved Brain Function

- **Neurogenesis**: Regular physical exercise promotes the growth of new neurons, particularly in the hippocampus, which is crucial for memory and learning.
- **Brain-Derived Neurotrophic Factor (BDNF)**: Exercise increases BDNF levels, supporting neuron growth and overall brain health.

Enhanced Cognitive Abilities

- **Improved Focus and Concentration**: Exercise boosts blood flow to the brain, enhancing focus, concentration, and mental alertness.
- **Better Memory**: Physical activity has been shown to improve memory retention and recall.

Example

- **Aerobic Exercise**: Activities like running, swimming, and cycling are particularly effective in boosting cognitive functions.

2. Nutrition and Mental Clarity

- **Omega-3 Fatty Acids**: Found in fish, flaxseeds, and walnuts, omega-3s are essential for brain health and cognitive function.
- **Antioxidants**: Foods rich in antioxidants (e.g., berries, dark chocolate) protect the brain from oxidative stress and improve mental clarity.

Stable Blood Sugar Levels

- **Balanced Diet**: Eating balanced meals helps maintain stable blood sugar levels, preventing energy crashes and promoting sustained mental focus.
- **Avoiding Processed Foods**: Reducing the intake of processed sugars and refined carbs prevents spikes and drops in blood sugar that can impair cognitive function.

Example

- **Mediterranean Diet**: Rich in fruits, vegetables, whole grains, and healthy fats, this diet is associated with better cognitive health and reduced risk of cognitive decline.

3. Sleep and Cognitive Performance

Restorative Sleep

- **Memory Consolidation**: During sleep, the brain consolidates memories and processes information from the day, enhancing learning and retention.
- **Cognitive Function**: Adequate sleep improves attention, problem-solving skills, and overall cognitive performance.

Sleep Hygiene

- **Consistent Schedule**: Maintaining a regular sleep schedule helps regulate the body's internal clock and improves sleep quality.
- **Sleep Environment**: A comfortable, dark, and quiet sleep environment promotes better sleep.

- **7-9 Hours of Sleep**: Most adults need 7-9 hours of sleep per night for optimal cognitive function and mental clarity.

4. Stress Management and Mental Clarity

Reducing Stress Through Physical Activity

- **Endorphin Release**: Exercise stimulates the release of endorphins, which are natural mood lifters that reduce stress and anxiety.
- **Cortisol Regulation**: Physical activity helps regulate cortisol levels, preventing the negative cognitive effects of chronic stress.

Mind-Body Practices

- **Yoga and Tai Chi**: These practices combine physical movement with mindfulness, reducing stress and enhancing mental clarity.

Example

- **Daily Exercise**: Incorporating daily physical activity, such as a brisk walk or yoga session, can significantly reduce stress levels and improve mental clarity.

5. Hydration and Cognitive Function

Maintaining Hydration

- **Brain Function**: Proper hydration is essential for maintaining concentration, alertness, and cognitive performance.
- **Preventing Fatigue**: Dehydration can lead to fatigue and decreased cognitive function.

Hydration Tips

- **Regular Water Intake**: Aim to drink water regularly throughout the day, especially during and after exercise.

- **Hydrating Foods**: Include water-rich foods like fruits and vegetables in your diet.

Example

- **8 Glasses a Day**: A common recommendation is to drink at least 8 glasses of water a day to maintain adequate hydration levels.

6. Mental Health and Physical Well-being

Physical Activity and Mental Health

- **Reduced Depression and Anxiety**: Regular physical activity is effective in reducing symptoms of depression and anxiety.
- **Improved Mood**: Exercise promotes the release of neurotransmitters like serotonin and dopamine, which improve mood and mental clarity.

Holistic Health

- **Mind-Body Connection**: Taking care of physical health through exercise, nutrition, and sleep positively impacts mental health and cognitive function.

Example

- **Integrated Routine**: A holistic approach that combines regular physical activity, a balanced diet, adequate sleep, and stress management techniques can significantly enhance mental clarity and overall well-being.

By maintaining good physical health through exercise, proper nutrition, adequate sleep, stress management, and hydration, you can enhance mental clarity, cognitive function, and overall psychological well-being. This interconnected approach ensures that both body and mind are optimized for peak performance.

Establishing habits for physical well-being: Exercise, nutrition, adequate sleep.

Establishing habits for physical well-being involves creating a sustainable routine that incorporates regular exercise, balanced nutrition, and adequate sleep. Here's a comprehensive guide on how to develop and maintain these habits:

1. Exercise

Creating an Exercise Routine

1. **Set Clear Goals**
   - **Specific**: Define what you want to achieve (e.g., run a 5K, build muscle, improve flexibility).
   - **Measurable**: Set quantifiable targets (e.g., exercise 4 times a week, lift a certain weight).
2. **Choose Activities You Enjoy**
   - **Variety**: Include different types of exercise like cardio, strength training, and flexibility exercises.
   - **Enjoyment**: Pick activities you find fun, such as dancing, hiking, swimming, or playing a sport.
3. **Start Small and Progress Gradually**
   - **Beginner-Friendly**: Start with manageable workouts and gradually increase intensity and duration.
   - **Consistency**: Aim for at least 150 minutes of moderate aerobic activity or 75 minutes of vigorous activity per week, combined with muscle-strengthening activities on two or more days a week.
4. **Schedule Your Workouts**
   - **Routine**: Set a specific time for exercise each day to make it a habit.
   - **Flexibility**: Have backup plans for rainy days or busy schedules, like indoor workouts or shorter sessions.

Example Routine

- **Monday**: 30-minute brisk walk or jog.

- **Wednesday**: 45-minute strength training session.
- **Friday**: 30-minute yoga or stretching routine.
- **Sunday**: 1-hour hike or bike ride.

2. Nutrition

Building Healthy Eating Habits

1. **Plan Balanced Meals**
   - **Macronutrients**: Ensure each meal includes a balance of carbohydrates, proteins, and healthy fats.
   - **Micronutrients**: Eat a variety of fruits and vegetables to get essential vitamins and minerals.
2. **Portion Control**
   - **Mindful Eating**: Be aware of portion sizes and listen to your body's hunger and fullness cues.
   - **Healthy Snacking**: Choose nutritious snacks like nuts, fruits, and yogurt.
3. **Stay Hydrated**
   - **Water Intake**: Aim for at least 8 glasses of water a day.
   - **Limit Sugary Drinks**: Reduce consumption of sodas, energy drinks, and other high-sugar beverages.
4. **Plan and Prepare Meals**
   - **Meal Prep**: Prepare meals in advance to ensure healthy choices are available.
   - **Grocery List**: Make a shopping list based on healthy meal plans to avoid impulse buys.

Example Daily Meal Plan

- **Breakfast**: Oatmeal with fresh berries and a tablespoon of almond butter.
- **Lunch**: Grilled chicken salad with mixed greens, cherry tomatoes, cucumber, and olive oil dressing.
- **Snack**: A handful of almonds and an apple.
- **Dinner**: Baked salmon, quinoa, and steamed broccoli.
- **Evening Snack**: Greek yogurt with a drizzle of honey.

3. Adequate Sleep

Establishing a Healthy Sleep Routine

1. **Set a Consistent Sleep Schedule**
   o **Regular Bedtime**: Go to bed and wake up at the same time every day, even on weekends.
   o **Wind Down Routine**: Create a relaxing pre-sleep routine, such as reading or taking a warm bath.
2. **Create a Sleep-Friendly Environment**
   o **Comfortable Bedding**: Invest in a comfortable mattress and pillows.
   o **Dark, Quiet, and Cool**: Ensure your bedroom is dark, quiet, and cool to promote better sleep.
3. **Limit Screen Time Before Bed**
   o **Reduce Blue Light Exposure**: Avoid screens at least an hour before bed to improve sleep quality.
   o **Relaxing Activities**: Engage in relaxing activities like meditation or listening to calming music.
4. **Be Mindful of Food and Drink**
   o **Avoid Caffeine and Heavy Meals**: Limit caffeine and avoid heavy meals close to bedtime.
   o **Hydration**: Drink water throughout the day but reduce intake close to bedtime to avoid waking up during the night.

Example Sleep Routine

- **9:00 PM**: Begin wind-down routine (dim lights, read a book).
- **9:30 PM**: Turn off electronic devices.
- **9:45 PM**: Practice relaxation techniques (deep breathing, gentle stretching).
- **10:00 PM**: Go to bed.

Tips for Sustaining Habits

1. **Set Realistic Goals**
   o **Achievable**: Start with small, achievable goals to build confidence and momentum.

- o **Adjustable**: Be flexible and adjust goals as needed to stay motivated.
2. **Track Your Progress**
   - o **Journal or Apps**: Use a journal or apps to track workouts, meals, and sleep patterns.
   - o **Reflect and Adjust**: Regularly review progress and make necessary adjustments to your routine.
3. **Seek Support and Accountability**
   - o **Support System**: Share your goals with friends, family, or join a community group.
   - o **Accountability Partner**: Find a workout buddy or a friend to keep each other motivated.
4. **Celebrate Successes**
   - o **Rewards**: Celebrate milestones and achievements with non-food rewards.
   - o **Positive Reinforcement**: Acknowledge your efforts and progress to stay motivated.

By establishing and maintaining these habits for physical well-being, you can improve your overall health, enhance your mental clarity, and increase your energy levels, ultimately leading to a more balanced and fulfilling life.

Mindfulness and stress management techniques to enhance resilience.

Mindfulness and stress management techniques are powerful tools to enhance resilience, helping individuals cope with challenges and bounce back from adversity. Here are several effective practices you can incorporate into your routine:

1. Mindfulness Techniques

1.1 Mindful Breathing

- **Purpose**: Focuses attention on the present moment, calming the mind and reducing stress.
- **Practice**: Sit quietly and observe your breath. Inhale deeply through your nose, hold briefly, and exhale slowly through your mouth. Repeat for several minutes.

1.2 Body Scan Meditation

- **Purpose**: Increases awareness of bodily sensations, promoting relaxation and reducing tension.
- **Practice**: Lie down or sit comfortably. Focus on each part of your body sequentially, from toes to head, noticing any sensations without judgment.

1.3 Mindful Eating

- **Purpose**: Enhances appreciation of food and aids digestion by focusing on the sensory experience.
- **Practice**: Eat slowly, savoring each bite. Notice textures, flavors, and how your body responds to each mouthful. Minimize distractions like screens or reading.

2. Stress Management Techniques

2.1 Progressive Muscle Relaxation (PMR)

- **Purpose**: Reduces muscle tension and promotes relaxation through systematic tensing and relaxing of muscle groups.
- **Practice**: Start with your feet and work your way up, tensing each muscle group for 5-10 seconds and then releasing. Focus on the contrast between tension and relaxation.

2.2 Deep Breathing Exercises

- **Purpose**: Calms the nervous system, lowers heart rate, and reduces stress hormones.

- **Practice**: Inhale deeply through your nose for a count of 4, hold for 4, exhale slowly through your mouth for 6-8 counts. Repeat several times.

2.3 Visualization and Guided Imagery

- **Purpose**: Uses mental imagery to create a sense of calm and positive outcomes.
- **Practice**: Close your eyes and imagine a peaceful place or visualize successfully overcoming a challenge. Engage all senses to make the visualization vivid.

3. Techniques to Enhance Resilience

3.1 Cognitive Reframing

- **Purpose**: Shifts perspective from negative to positive interpretations of stressful events, promoting resilience.
- **Practice**: Identify negative thoughts related to a challenge. Challenge them by considering alternative perspectives or potential positive outcomes.

3.2 Gratitude Practice

- **Purpose**: Cultivates positivity and resilience by focusing on what you're thankful for, even in difficult times.
- **Practice**: Keep a gratitude journal. Each day, write down three things you're grateful for, no matter how small.

3.3 Social Support and Connection

- **Purpose**: Strengthens resilience by providing emotional support and fostering a sense of belonging.

- **Practice**: Maintain relationships with supportive friends and family. Seek out social activities or groups that share your interests.

Integration into Daily Routine

- **Consistency**: Practice mindfulness and stress management techniques daily to build resilience over time.
- **Adaptation**: Adjust techniques based on your needs and preferences. Experiment with different practices to find what works best for you.
- **Mindful Breaks**: Incorporate short mindfulness practices throughout the day, such as mindful breathing during breaks at work or before challenging tasks.

By integrating these mindfulness and stress management techniques into your daily routine, you can enhance your resilience, manage stress effectively, and cultivate a greater sense of well-being even during challenging times. Regular practice will strengthen your ability to bounce back from setbacks and maintain emotional balance.

Chapter 6: Continuous Learning and Growth

- The importance of lifelong learning in personal and professional development.
- Daily habits for learning: Reading, listening to podcasts, taking online courses.
- Cultivating a growth mindset: Embracing challenges and setbacks as opportunities for growth.

The importance of lifelong learning in personal and professional development.

Lifelong learning plays a crucial role in both personal and professional development, offering continuous growth, adaptability, and fulfillment throughout one's life. Here are several key reasons why lifelong learning is essential:

1. Adaptability to Change

- **Continuous Skill Development**: In today's rapidly evolving world, skills become outdated quickly. Lifelong learning allows individuals to adapt to technological advancements, industry changes, and new methodologies.
- **Flexibility**: Learning new skills or knowledge areas enhances flexibility in career paths and personal pursuits, enabling individuals to pivot when necessary.

2. Career Advancement

- **Competitive Edge**: Continuous learning keeps knowledge and skills relevant, making individuals more competitive in the job market.
- **Promotion Opportunities**: Employers value employees who demonstrate a commitment to learning and growth, often leading to increased responsibilities and career advancement.

3. Personal Growth and Fulfillment

- **Intellectual Stimulation**: Learning new subjects or skills stimulates the mind, enhancing cognitive function and creativity.
- **Personal Enrichment**: Exploring diverse topics fosters personal interests and passions, contributing to a more enriched and satisfying life.

4. Keeping Up with Industry Trends

- **Professional Relevance**: Lifelong learning ensures professionals stay informed about industry trends, best practices, and emerging technologies.
- **Networking Opportunities**: Participation in workshops, seminars, and online courses facilitates networking with peers and industry leaders, fostering professional relationships and collaborations.

5. Problem-Solving and Critical Thinking

- **Analytical Skills**: Continual learning sharpens problem-solving abilities and critical thinking skills, enabling individuals to approach challenges with confidence and creativity.
- **Innovation**: Exposure to new ideas and perspectives encourages innovative thinking, leading to novel solutions in both personal and professional contexts.

6. Personal Development and Well-being

- **Self-Confidence**: Acquiring new knowledge and skills boosts self-confidence and self-esteem, empowering individuals to set and achieve ambitious goals.
- **Resilience**: Lifelong learners are better equipped to navigate uncertainties and setbacks, viewing challenges as opportunities for growth rather than obstacles.

Strategies for Lifelong Learning

- **Formal Education**: Pursue higher education, certifications, or specialized courses relevant to your field or interests.
- **Informal Learning**: Read books, articles, and blogs; listen to podcasts; attend webinars; and participate in online communities.
- **Skill Development**: Practice new skills through hands-on projects, workshops, or mentorship programs.
- **Networking**: Engage in professional associations, conferences, and industry events to stay connected and informed.

By embracing lifelong learning, individuals foster personal growth, career advancement, and adaptability in an ever-changing world. It's a mindset that promotes continuous improvement and resilience, ultimately leading to a more fulfilling and successful life journey.

Daily habits for learning: Reading, listening to podcasts, taking online courses.

Daily habits for learning are essential for continuous growth and development. Here are effective habits you can incorporate into your routine to enhance your learning:

1. Reading

- **Knowledge Acquisition**: Reading exposes you to new ideas, information, and perspectives.
- **Critical Thinking**: Engaging with books improves analytical skills and enhances cognitive abilities.

Habits

- **Set Aside Time**: Dedicate a specific time each day for reading, even if it's just 15-30 minutes.
- **Choose Diverse Topics**: Read books across different genres and subjects to broaden your understanding.
- **Take Notes**: Jot down key points, insights, and questions for further exploration.

Example

- **Morning Routine**: Read a chapter of a non-fiction book related to your career or personal interests before starting your day.

2. Listening to Podcasts

Purpose

- **Convenient Learning**: Podcasts provide accessible knowledge on various topics while multitasking (e.g., commuting, exercising).
- **Expert Insights**: Listen to industry experts and thought leaders share their experiences and expertise.

Habits

- **Curate a Playlist**: Subscribe to podcasts that cover topics aligned with your professional goals or personal interests.
- **Daily Listening**: Incorporate podcast listening into daily routines, such as during workouts, cooking, or commuting.
- **Reflect and Apply**: Take notes on key takeaways and ideas to apply them in your work or personal life.

- **Commute**: Listen to a business or educational podcast episode during your daily commute to stay informed and inspired.

3. Taking Online Courses

Purpose

- **Skill Development**: Online courses offer structured learning opportunities to acquire new skills or deepen existing ones.
- **Flexibility**: Learn at your own pace and schedule, fitting courses around your daily commitments.

Habits

- **Set Learning Goals**: Identify specific skills or knowledge areas you want to develop through online courses.
- **Allocate Time**: Dedicate consistent time blocks for coursework, whether daily or weekly.
- **Engage Actively**: Complete assignments, participate in forums, and apply learned concepts to real-world projects.

Example

- **Lunch Break**: Use your lunch hour to watch a video lesson or complete a module of an online course.

4. Reflective Practice

Purpose

- **Integration of Learning**: Reflecting on daily learning experiences enhances retention and understanding.
- **Continuous Improvement**: Identify areas for further exploration or skills that require reinforcement.

- **Journaling**: Write brief reflections on what you learned each day, including insights gained and ideas for application.
- **Review Goals**: Regularly revisit your learning goals and track progress made through your daily habits.
- **Adjust and Adapt**: Modify your learning habits based on what works best for you and where you need improvement.

Example

- **Evening Ritual**: Spend 10-15 minutes reflecting on the day's reading, podcast listening, or course materials in a journal.

Tips for Sustaining Learning Habits

- **Consistency**: Make learning a daily habit by integrating it into your routine at consistent times.
- **Variety**: Explore different formats and sources of learning to keep engagement high and avoid monotony.
- **Accountability**: Share your learning goals with a friend or join online communities to stay motivated and accountable.

By cultivating these daily habits for learning, you foster continuous personal and professional growth, stay informed about industry trends, and develop valuable skills that contribute to your success and fulfillment.

Cultivating a growth mindset: Embracing challenges and setbacks as opportunities for growth

Cultivating a growth mindset involves embracing challenges and setbacks as opportunities for learning and development rather than viewing them as obstacles. Here's how you can foster and maintain a growth mindset:

1. Understanding the Growth Mindset

- **Belief in Potential**: Embrace the belief that abilities and intelligence can be developed through dedication and hard work.
- **Resilience**: See setbacks and failures as temporary setbacks that provide valuable feedback and opportunities for improvement.

2. Embracing Challenges

Purpose

- **Opportunities for Growth**: Challenges provide chances to stretch your abilities and learn new skills.
- **Building Resilience**: Overcoming challenges strengthens your ability to persevere in the face of adversity.

Practices

- **Set Goals**: Establish challenging yet attainable goals that push you out of your comfort zone.
- **Seek Feedback**: Use feedback from challenges to identify areas for improvement and adjust your approach.

Example

- **Professional Development**: Take on projects or tasks that require you to learn new skills or tackle complex problems.

3. Viewing Setbacks as Learning Opportunities

Purpose

- **Iterative Improvement**: See setbacks as natural parts of the learning process rather than indications of failure.
- **Adaptability**: Learn from setbacks to refine strategies and approaches for future endeavors.

- **Reflective Practice**: Analyze setbacks objectively, identifying factors within your control and areas for adjustment.
- **Mindfulness**: Maintain a positive outlook by focusing on what you've learned and how setbacks contribute to your growth.

Example

- **Career Development**: If a project doesn't go as planned, analyze what went wrong, gather insights, and apply them to future projects.

4. Continuous Learning and Development

Purpose

- **Lifelong Growth**: Cultivate a mindset of continuous improvement and learning.
- **Adaptability**: Stay current with industry trends and innovations by actively seeking new knowledge and skills.

Practices

- **Skill Acquisition**: Pursue learning opportunities through courses, workshops, and self-study.
- **Feedback Loop**: Regularly assess progress, adjust goals, and celebrate achievements to maintain motivation and momentum.

Example

- **Personal Growth**: Dedicate time each day to learn something new, whether through reading, online courses, or podcasts.

5. Building Resilience and Confidence

Purpose

- **Confidence**: Develop self-assurance in your ability to overcome challenges and achieve goals.
- **Perseverance**: Strengthen resilience to bounce back from setbacks with renewed determination.

Practices

- **Positive Self-Talk**: Replace negative thoughts with affirmations that reinforce your ability to learn and grow.
- **Role Models**: Draw inspiration from individuals who exemplify a growth mindset and learn from their experiences.

Example

- **Personal Challenges**: Engage in hobbies or activities where you're not initially proficient, such as learning a new language or musical instrument.

Tips for Cultivating a Growth Mindset

- **Challenge Yourself**: Seek out opportunities that push you beyond your current abilities.
- **Celebrate Effort**: Focus on the process and effort invested rather than solely on outcomes.
- **Learn from Criticism**: Use constructive feedback to improve and refine your skills.
- **Surround Yourself**: Surround yourself with supportive individuals who encourage growth and learning.

By embracing challenges and setbacks as opportunities for growth, you cultivate a resilient mindset that empowers you to achieve greater success and fulfillment in both personal and professional endeavors.

Chapter 7: Building Relationships and Networks

- The value of networking and fostering meaningful relationships.
- Daily habits for effective communication and relationship building.
- Strategies for expanding your professional network and leveraging it for success.

The value of networking and fostering meaningful relationships

Networking and fostering meaningful relationships are invaluable for personal growth, career advancement, and overall well-being. Here's a detailed look at their importance:

1. Professional Advancement

- **Opportunities**: Networking expands your professional circle, increasing access to job opportunities, mentorship, and career advice.

- **Career Development**: Relationships with industry peers and mentors provide insights into industry trends, best practices, and potential career paths.
- **Referrals**: Strong networks often lead to referrals for job openings or projects, enhancing career prospects.

2. Knowledge and Information Sharing

- **Learning Opportunities**: Engaging with diverse perspectives and experiences through networking enriches your knowledge base.
- **Innovation**: Discussions with peers can spark innovative ideas and solutions to challenges within your field or industry.

3. Personal Growth

- **Support System**: Meaningful relationships offer emotional support during professional transitions, setbacks, and successes.
- **Feedback**: Honest feedback from trusted contacts helps you identify blind spots and areas for improvement.

4. Building Confidence and Visibility

- **Self-Promotion**: Networking allows you to showcase your skills, accomplishments, and expertise, boosting confidence in your abilities.
- **Recognition**: Building a positive reputation among peers and industry leaders enhances visibility and opens doors to new opportunities.

5. Collaboration and Teamwork

- **Synergy**: Collaborating with individuals from diverse backgrounds fosters creativity and enhances problem-solving capabilities.

- **Resource Sharing**: Networking facilitates access to resources, such as specialized knowledge, tools, or funding, for collaborative projects.

Strategies for Effective Networking

- **Attend Events**: Participate in industry conferences, seminars, and workshops to meet professionals with similar interests.
- **Online Platforms**: Utilize social media platforms like LinkedIn to connect with professionals, join groups, and engage in discussions.
- **Follow Up**: Maintain relationships by following up with contacts, offering assistance, and staying in touch through periodic communication.

Cultivating Meaningful Relationships

- **Authenticity**: Build relationships based on mutual respect, trust, and genuine interest in others' success.
- **Reciprocity**: Offer support, advice, and resources to your network, fostering a culture of reciprocity and collaboration.
- **Long-term Investment**: Nurture relationships over time by staying connected, celebrating milestones, and offering ongoing support.

Personal and Professional Benefits

Networking and fostering meaningful relationships not only enhance career opportunities and professional growth but also contribute to personal fulfillment and well-being. By investing in relationships and actively participating in networking activities, you create a supportive community that enriches both your personal and professional life.

Daily habits for effective communication and relationship building.

Effective communication and relationship building are foundational skills that can be cultivated through daily habits. Here are some key habits to enhance your communication skills and build meaningful relationships:

1. Active Listening

- **Purpose**: Understand others' perspectives, build trust, and foster deeper connections.
- **Habits**:
    - **Focus**: Pay full attention to the speaker without interrupting or planning your response.
    - **Empathy**: Put yourself in the speaker's shoes to understand their emotions and motivations.
    - **Clarification**: Ask open-ended questions and paraphrase to ensure you grasp the speaker's message accurately.

2. Practicing Empathy

- **Purpose**: Strengthen relationships by demonstrating understanding and support.
- **Habits**:
    - **Reflection**: Reflect on others' feelings and experiences to validate their emotions.
    - **Validation**: Acknowledge and respect differing viewpoints, even if you don't agree.
    - **Support**: Offer help or encouragement when someone is facing challenges or difficulties.

3. Clear and Concise Communication

- **Purpose**: Avoid misunderstandings and convey information effectively.
- **Habits**:

- Structure: Organize your thoughts before speaking or writing to maintain clarity.
- Simplicity: Use simple language and avoid jargon to ensure your message is easily understood.
- Feedback: Encourage feedback to ensure your message has been received as intended.

4. Building Trust and Rapport

- **Purpose**: Create a foundation for meaningful relationships and collaboration.
- **Habits**:
  - Consistency: Follow through on commitments and be reliable in your interactions.
  - Transparency: Share information openly and honestly, maintaining integrity.
  - Respect: Show respect for others' opinions and boundaries to foster mutual trust.

5. Non-verbal Communication Awareness

- **Purpose**: Enhance understanding and convey messages effectively through body language and facial expressions.
- **Habits**:
  - Eye Contact: Maintain appropriate eye contact to show engagement and attentiveness.
  - Posture: Adopt open and relaxed body language to convey approachability and confidence.
  - Facial Expressions: Use facial expressions to reinforce your message and convey emotions authentically.

6. Regular Feedback and Reflection

- **Purpose**: Continuously improve communication skills and strengthen relationships.

- **Habits**:
  - ○ **Seek Feedback**: Ask for feedback from colleagues, friends, or mentors on your communication style.
  - ○ **Self-Reflection**: Reflect on your interactions daily to identify areas for improvement.
  - ○ **Learning**: Learn from each communication experience to refine your approach and skills.

Example Daily Habits

- **Morning Reflection**: Spend a few minutes reviewing upcoming meetings or conversations, preparing mentally to listen actively and communicate effectively.
- **Daily Check-ins**: Schedule brief check-ins with team members or colleagues to discuss progress, challenges, and goals, practicing empathy and clear communication.
- **Evening Review**: Reflect on your communication throughout the day, noting successes and areas for improvement, and set goals for tomorrow's interactions.

By incorporating these daily habits into your routine, you can strengthen your communication skills, build meaningful relationships, and foster a positive and collaborative environment in both personal and professional settings.

Strategies for expanding your professional network and leveraging it for success

Expanding your professional network and leveraging it for success involves strategic planning, consistent effort, and genuine relationship-building. Here are effective strategies to help you expand and utilize your network effectively:

1. Networking Strategies

- **Attend Industry Events**: Participate in conferences, seminars, trade shows, and networking events relevant to your field.
- **Join Professional Associations**: Become a member of industry-specific organizations and attend their meetings and networking gatherings.
- **Utilize Online Platforms**: Use LinkedIn and other social media platforms to connect with professionals in your industry, join relevant groups, and engage in discussions.
- **Alumni Networks**: Leverage your alumni associations for networking opportunities, mentorship, and career advice.
- **Informational Interviews**: Request informational interviews with professionals in roles or industries of interest to expand your network and gain insights.

2. Building Relationships

- **Focus on Quality**: Prioritize building genuine, meaningful relationships over simply collecting contacts.
- **Offer Value**: Seek opportunities to help others by sharing knowledge, resources, or introductions.
- **Stay Connected**: Regularly follow up with your contacts to maintain relationships and stay top-of-mind.
- **Attend Networking Follow-ups**: Attend post-event networking sessions or informal gatherings to deepen connections made at events.
- **Be Authentic**: Show genuine interest in others' work and career goals, and be transparent about your own objectives.

3. Leveraging Your Network for Success

- **Seek Mentorship**: Identify mentors within your network who can provide guidance, advice, and support in your career development.
- **Referrals and Recommendations**: Ask for referrals and recommendations from trusted contacts when seeking new opportunities or collaborations.

- **Collaborations and Partnerships**: Explore collaborative projects or partnerships with professionals in your network to leverage complementary skills and expand your capabilities.
- **Professional Development**: Utilize your network to stay informed about industry trends, new opportunities, and professional development resources.
- **Job Opportunities**: Inform your network of your career aspirations and actively seek out job opportunities that may be shared within your network.

4. Networking Etiquette and Best Practices

- **Follow Up Promptly**: Send a thank-you note or email after networking events or meetings to express appreciation and reinforce connections.
- **Offer Assistance**: Be willing to assist others in your network without expecting immediate reciprocation.
- **Maintain Professionalism**: Conduct yourself professionally at all times, respecting confidentiality and boundaries within your network.
- **Stay Organized**: Use tools or systems to manage and track your networking contacts, interactions, and follow-ups.
- **Continuous Engagement**: Regularly update your network on your achievements, projects, and milestones to keep them engaged and supportive.

Example Networking Action Plan

- **Week 1**: Attend a local industry meetup and connect with at least three new professionals.
- **Week 2**: Schedule informational interviews with two professionals in roles you aspire to learn more about.
- **Week 3**: Join a LinkedIn group related to your field and participate in discussions.
- **Week 4**: Offer to assist a colleague or contact with a project or introduction, demonstrating your value to your network.

By implementing these strategies consistently and authentically, you can effectively expand your professional network, cultivate valuable relationships, and leverage them to achieve your career goals and success.

Chapter 8: Reflection and Adaptation

- The role of self-reflection in evaluating progress and adjusting course.
- Daily practices for self-assessment and course correction.
- Celebrating successes and learning from failures to fuel continuous improvement

The role of self-reflection in evaluating progress and adjusting course.

Self-reflection plays a crucial role in personal and professional development by providing opportunities to assess progress, identify areas for improvement, and make necessary adjustments. Here's how self-reflection contributes to evaluating progress and adjusting course effectively:

1. Assessing Goals and Objectives

- **Clarity**: Reflecting allows you to clarify your goals, ensuring they are specific, measurable, achievable, relevant, and time-bound (SMART).
- **Alignment**: Evaluate whether your current actions and strategies align with your long-term objectives and aspirations.
- **Progress Tracking**: Measure progress toward your goals by reviewing achievements, milestones reached, and challenges overcome.

2. Identifying Strengths and Weaknesses

- **Self-Awareness**: Gain insights into your strengths, weaknesses, and areas needing improvement through honest self-assessment.
- **Feedback Incorporation**: Integrate feedback received from others into your self-reflection to gain a comprehensive view of your performance.

3. Learning from Experiences

- **Lessons Learned**: Analyze successes and setbacks to extract valuable lessons and insights.
- **Adaptability**: Use reflections to adapt strategies, approaches, and behaviors based on past experiences and outcomes.

4. Enhancing Decision-Making

- **Critical Thinking**: Develop critical thinking skills by evaluating decisions made and their impact on progress.
- **Course Correction**: Identify opportunities for course correction or adjustment to optimize future actions and outcomes.

5. Personal Growth and Development

- **Continuous Improvement**: Foster a growth mindset by continuously striving for improvement and learning from experiences.
- **Self-Motivation**: Stay motivated by celebrating achievements and acknowledging progress made, no matter how small.

Strategies for Effective Self-Reflection

- **Regular Practice**: Dedicate time regularly, such as daily or weekly, for self-reflection to maintain awareness and track progress.

- **Journaling**: Write down thoughts, observations, achievements, challenges, and lessons learned to facilitate deeper introspection.
- **Feedback Solicitation**: Seek feedback from mentors, colleagues, or trusted individuals to gain different perspectives and insights.
- **Goal Review**: Regularly review and update goals based on self-reflection to ensure they remain relevant and aligned with your aspirations.
- **Action Planning**: Develop action plans based on insights gained from self-reflection to implement changes and improvements effectively.

Example Self-Reflection Process

- **Set Aside Time**: Allocate 15-30 minutes at the end of each week to reflect on achievements, challenges faced, and lessons learned.
- **Review Goals**: Assess progress toward weekly or monthly goals, noting accomplishments and areas needing further development.
- **Identify Patterns**: Recognize recurring patterns in behaviors or decision-making that may impact progress or effectiveness.
- **Plan Adjustments**: Based on insights gained, adjust strategies, set new priorities, or seek additional support or resources as needed.

By integrating self-reflection into your routine, you can enhance self-awareness, optimize decision-making, and foster continuous growth and development in both personal and professional aspects of your life.

Daily practices for self-assessment and course correction.

Daily practices for self-assessment and course correction are essential for maintaining progress, adapting to challenges, and achieving goals effectively. Here are practical daily habits you can implement to facilitate self-assessment and course correction:

1. Morning Review and Planning

- **Purpose**: Set the tone for the day, align actions with goals, and anticipate challenges.
- **Habits**:

  - **Review Goals**: Reflect on your short-term and long-term goals.
  - **Prioritize Tasks**: Identify key tasks for the day based on your goals and priorities.
  - **Anticipate Challenges**: Consider potential obstacles and strategize how to overcome them.

2. Regular Check-ins Throughout the Day

- **Purpose**: Maintain focus, monitor progress, and adjust priorities as needed.
- **Habits**:
  - **Progress Tracking**: Periodically assess your progress on tasks and projects.
  - **Time Management**: Evaluate how effectively you're managing your time and adjust your schedule if necessary.
  - **Stay Flexible**: Be prepared to adapt to unexpected changes or new information that may impact your plans.

3. End-of-Day Reflection

- **Purpose**: Review accomplishments, identify areas for improvement, and plan for the next day.
- **Habits**:

- o **Review Achievements**: Acknowledge and celebrate accomplishments for the day.
- o **Assess Challenges**: Reflect on challenges encountered and lessons learned.
- o **Adjust Goals**: Evaluate whether daily goals were achieved and adjust priorities or tasks for the following day accordingly.

4. Weekly or Biweekly Progress Reviews

- **Purpose**: Gain a broader perspective on your overall progress toward long-term goals.
- **Habits**:
  - o **Goal Alignment**: Assess whether your daily actions are aligned with your weekly or monthly objectives.
  - o **Course Correction**: Identify any trends or recurring issues that may require adjustments in your approach.
  - o **Celebrate Milestones**: Recognize and celebrate milestones reached over the past week or two.

5. Feedback Solicitation

- **Purpose**: Gather insights from others to gain different perspectives and identify blind spots.
- **Habits**:
  - o **Seek Feedback**: Regularly ask for feedback from colleagues, mentors, or trusted individuals.
  - o **Open Communication**: Maintain open communication to receive constructive criticism and suggestions for improvement.
  - o **Reflect and Apply**: Integrate feedback into your self-assessment process and adjust your strategies accordingly.

Example Daily Self-Assessment Routine

- **Morning**: Review goals and prioritize tasks for the day during a brief planning session.

- **Throughout the Day**: Check in periodically to assess progress and adjust priorities based on changing circumstances.
- **Evening**: Reflect on achievements, challenges faced, and lessons learned during an end-of-day review.
- **Weekly**: Conduct a more thorough review of progress toward weekly goals, adjust plans as needed, and seek feedback from peers or mentors.

By consistently practicing these daily habits for self-assessment and course correction, you can enhance productivity, maintain alignment with your goals, and continuously improve your effectiveness in achieving desired outcomes.

Celebrating successes and learning from failures to fuel continuous improvement

Celebrating successes and learning from failures are essential practices that fuel continuous improvement and growth. Here's how you can effectively incorporate these elements into your personal and professional life:

Celebrating Successes

Celebrating successes is crucial for maintaining motivation, boosting morale, and reinforcing positive behaviors and achievements. Here are ways to effectively celebrate your successes:

1. **Acknowledge Achievements**: Take time to recognize and appreciate your accomplishments, whether big or small.
2. **Reflect on Progress**: Reflect on how far you've come and the efforts that contributed to your success.
3. **Reward Yourself**: Treat yourself to something special or engage in activities that bring you joy as a reward for your hard work.

4. **Share Successes**: Share your achievements with others, such as friends, family, or colleagues, to celebrate together and build a supportive network.
5. **Set New Goals**: Use your success as momentum to set new, challenging goals that build upon your achievements.

Learning from Failures

Failure is a natural part of growth and provides valuable lessons that can lead to future success. Here's how you can effectively learn from failures:

1. **Embrace Failure as a Learning Opportunity**: Shift your perspective to view failures as opportunities for growth and learning.
2. **Reflect and Analyze**: Take time to reflect on what went wrong, identify factors within your control, and analyze lessons learned.
3. **Adjust Strategies**: Use insights gained from failure to adjust your strategies, approaches, or behaviors for future endeavors.
4. **Seek Feedback**: Ask for feedback from trusted individuals to gain different perspectives and insights on areas for improvement.
5. **Persist and Adapt**: Maintain resilience and perseverance, applying lessons learned to overcome setbacks and challenges.

Integrating Both Practices for Continuous Improvement

- **Balance**: Strike a balance between celebrating successes to maintain motivation and learning from failures to foster resilience and growth.
- **Feedback Loop**: Create a feedback loop where successes and failures are opportunities for reflection, adjustment, and improvement.

- **Mindset**: Cultivate a growth mindset that embraces challenges, values effort, and sees setbacks as stepping stones toward achieving long-term goals.

Example Practice

- **Weekly Reflection**: Schedule time each week to reflect on both successes and failures. Celebrate achievements and milestones reached, and analyze failures to extract lessons learned and identify areas for improvement.

By celebrating successes and learning from failures, you foster a culture of continuous improvement and personal growth. These practices not only enhance your effectiveness and resilience but also contribute to long-term success and fulfillment in both your personal and professional endeavors.

Chapter 8: Reflection and Adaptation

- The role of self-reflection in evaluating progress and adjusting course.
- Daily practices for self-assessment and course correction.
- Celebrating successes and learning from failures to fuel continuous improvement.

The role of self-reflection in evaluating progress and adjusting course

Self-reflection plays a crucial role in evaluating progress and adjusting course by providing a structured approach to introspect, assess, and make informed decisions about your actions and goals. Here's how self-reflection contributes to this process:

1. Assessment of Goals and Objectives

- **Clarity**: Self-reflection helps clarify your goals and objectives by examining whether they are still aligned with your values, priorities, and long-term aspirations.
- **Measurement**: It allows you to measure progress towards your goals, identifying what has been achieved and what still needs attention or adjustment.
- **Relevance**: Evaluate the relevance of your goals in the current context, ensuring they continue to motivate and guide your actions.

2. Identification of Strengths and Weaknesses

- **Self-Awareness**: Through reflection, you gain self-awareness by recognizing your strengths, weaknesses, and areas for improvement.
- **Feedback Integration**: Integrate feedback received from others into your self-assessment, gaining a holistic view of your performance and impact.
- **Skill Development**: Identify areas where additional skills or knowledge are needed to enhance your effectiveness in achieving goals.

3. Learning from Experiences

- **Lessons Learned**: Reflecting on experiences—both successes and setbacks—helps extract valuable lessons that inform future actions.

- **Adaptability**: Use insights gained from past experiences to adapt strategies, approaches, and behaviors, ensuring they align with your evolving circumstances and goals.
- **Continuous Improvement**: Foster a mindset of continuous improvement by actively seeking opportunities to learn and grow from every experience.

4. Decision-Making and Course Correction

- **Critical Analysis**: Self-reflection enables critical analysis of decisions made and their outcomes, identifying what worked well and what could be improved.
- **Adjustment**: Based on your assessment, adjust your course by revising goals, refining strategies, or realigning priorities to stay on track towards achieving desired outcomes.
- **Flexibility**: Maintain flexibility to adapt to unforeseen challenges or opportunities, responding proactively rather than reactively.

5. Personal Growth and Development

- **Self-Directed Learning**: Use self-reflection as a tool for self-directed learning, continuously seeking knowledge and skills that contribute to your growth.
- **Motivation**: Stay motivated and focused by celebrating achievements and milestones reached through your efforts.
- **Resilience**: Develop resilience by learning from setbacks and maintaining a positive outlook towards overcoming challenges.

Strategies for Effective Self-Reflection

- **Routine Practice**: Allocate dedicated time daily, weekly, or monthly for self-reflection to ensure consistency and regularity.
- **Journaling**: Keep a reflective journal to document thoughts, observations, achievements, challenges, and lessons learned.

- **Feedback Loop**: Incorporate feedback from mentors, colleagues, or trusted individuals to gain different perspectives and insights.
- **Goal Review**: Regularly review and update goals based on self-reflection to ensure they remain relevant and meaningful.

Example Self-Reflection Process

- **Set Aside Time**: Dedicate 15-30 minutes at the end of each day or week to reflect on your actions, progress, and achievements.
- **Ask Reflective Questions**: Consider questions like "What did I accomplish today/this week?", "What challenges did I face?", "What have I learned?", and "How can I improve?"
- **Plan Adjustments**: Based on your reflections, adjust your daily routines, priorities, or strategies to better align with your goals and aspirations.

By integrating self-reflection into your routine, you cultivate self-awareness, enhance decision-making abilities, and foster continuous growth and improvement in both personal and professional aspects of your life.

Daily practices for self-assessment and course correction.

Daily practices for self-assessment and course correction are essential for staying on track with your goals, adapting to changes, and continuously improving. Here are practical habits you can incorporate into your daily routine:

1. Morning Check-in and Planning

- **Purpose**: Set intentions for the day and align actions with your goals.
- **Habits**:
  - **Review Goals**: Start your day by reviewing your short-term and long-term goals.
  - **Prioritize Tasks**: Identify the most important tasks that will contribute to your goals.
  - **Visualize Success**: Imagine successfully completing your tasks and achieving your daily objectives.

2. Regular Progress Assessments

- **Purpose**: Monitor your progress throughout the day to ensure you're staying on track.
- **Habits**:
  - **Check-in Periodically**: Set aside brief moments to assess how your tasks are progressing.
  - **Evaluate Time Management**: Reflect on how effectively you're managing your time and adjust your schedule if needed.
  - **Course Correction**: Be ready to adapt to unexpected developments or new information that may require you to adjust your plans.

3. End-of-Day Reflection

- **Purpose**: Reflect on achievements, challenges faced, and lessons learned.
- **Habits**:
  - **Review Accomplishments**: Acknowledge what you've accomplished during the day.
  - **Assess Challenges**: Identify obstacles encountered and reflect on how you handled them.
  - **Learn from Experiences**: Extract lessons from both successes and failures to inform future actions.

4. Feedback Integration

- **Purpose**: Incorporate feedback from others to gain different perspectives and insights.
- **Habits**:
    - **Seek Feedback**: Regularly ask for feedback from mentors, colleagues, or trusted individuals.
    - **Open Communication**: Maintain open communication to receive constructive criticism and suggestions for improvement.
    - **Apply Insights**: Integrate feedback into your self-assessment process and adjust your strategies accordingly.

5. Weekly Review and Adjustment

- **Purpose**: Take a broader look at your progress and make adjustments for the upcoming week.
- **Habits**:
    - **Goal Alignment**: Evaluate whether your daily actions are aligned with your weekly or monthly objectives.
    - **Identify Trends**: Identify any recurring challenges or patterns that may require adjustments in your approach.
    - **Plan for Improvement**: Set new goals or adjust existing ones based on insights gained from daily assessments.

Example Daily Self-Assessment Routine

- **Morning**: Set aside 10-15 minutes to review goals, prioritize tasks, and visualize success for the day.
- **Throughout the Day**: Check in periodically between tasks to assess progress and adjust priorities as needed.
- **Evening**: Spend 15-20 minutes reflecting on accomplishments, challenges, and lessons learned from the day.

- **Weekly**: Dedicate an hour at the end of the week for a more comprehensive review, adjusting goals and strategies for the upcoming week based on your reflections.

By implementing these daily practices for self-assessment and course correction, you can enhance your productivity, maintain alignment with your goals, and continuously improve your effectiveness in achieving desired outcomes. These habits foster a proactive approach to personal and professional growth, ensuring you stay adaptable and responsive to changes and challenges.

Celebrating successes and learning from failures to fuel continuous improvement

Celebrating successes and learning from failures are integral parts of personal and professional growth. Here's how you can effectively incorporate both into your routine to fuel continuous improvement:

Celebrating Successes

Celebrating successes is essential for maintaining motivation, boosting morale, and reinforcing positive behaviors. Here are some effective practices:

1. **Acknowledge Achievements**: Take time to recognize and appreciate your accomplishments, no matter how small.
2. **Reflect on Progress**: Reflect on the journey that led to your success and the efforts you put in to achieve your goals.
3. **Reward Yourself**: Treat yourself to something special or engage in activities that you enjoy as a reward for your hard work and dedication.
4. **Share with Others**: Share your achievements with friends, family, or colleagues to celebrate together and build a supportive network.

5. **Set New Goals**: Use your success as momentum to set new, challenging goals that will continue to drive your growth and development.

Learning from Failures

Failure is a natural part of learning and provides valuable lessons that can lead to future success. Here's how you can effectively learn from failures:

1. **Embrace Failure as a Learning Opportunity**: Shift your mindset to view failures as opportunities for growth and development.
2. **Reflect and Analyze**: Take time to reflect on what went wrong, why it happened, and what you can learn from the experience.
3. **Identify Lessons Learned**: Extract valuable lessons and insights from your failures that can help you avoid similar mistakes in the future.
4. **Adapt and Adjust**: Use the lessons learned to adjust your approach, strategies, or behaviors to improve future outcomes.
5. **Seek Feedback**: Ask for feedback from mentors, colleagues, or trusted individuals to gain different perspectives and insights on what can be improved.

Integrating Both Practices for Continuous Improvement

- **Balance**: Find a balance between celebrating successes to maintain motivation and learning from failures to foster resilience and growth.
- **Feedback Loop**: Create a feedback loop where successes and failures are opportunities for reflection, adjustment, and improvement.
- **Mindset**: Cultivate a growth mindset that embraces challenges, values effort, and sees setbacks as opportunities for learning and improvement.

Example Practice

- **Weekly Reflection**: Dedicate time each week to reflect on both successes and failures. Celebrate achievements and milestones reached, and analyze failures to extract lessons learned and identify areas for improvement.

By celebrating successes and learning from failures, you foster a culture of continuous improvement and personal growth. These practices not only enhance your effectiveness and resilience but also contribute to long-term success and fulfillment in both your personal and professional endeavors.

Conclusion: Success is not a destination but a journey shaped by the habits we cultivate each day. By implementing the strategies and habits outlined in this eBook, you can create a foundation for sustainable success in all areas of your life. Remember, small daily actions lead to significant long-term results. Start today and watch your progress unfold!